# Ace Raider of the Unfathomable Universe

Also by Toni Thomas:

*Chosen*
    Brick Road Poetry Press

*Fast as Lightening*
    Gribble Press

*Walking on Water*
    Finishing Line Press

*Blue Halo*
    Annalese Press

# Ace Raider of the Unfathomable Universe

Toni Thomas

First published in 2016 by Annalese Press
134 Towngate
Netherthong
Holmfirth
West Yorkshire HD9 3XZ
England

Copyright © 2016 Toni Thomas

Please Note
All characters and situations appearing
in these pages are in the service of poetry.
Any resemblance to real persons,
living or dead, is purely coincidental.

All rights reserved. No part of this publication may be reproduced, stored, or transmitted in any form, or by any means electronic, mechanical or photocopying, recording or otherwise, without the express written permission of the publisher.

Cover artwork by Peter Wadsworth

*British Library Cataloguing-in-Publication Data*
A catalogue record for this book is available on request from the British Library.

ISBN 978-0-9956652-0-0

for Steve

## Acknowledgements

My deep gratitude goes to not only the amazing world class poets I have been very fortunate to work with, but also to the personal friends who have shown me endless support and encouragement and ultimately made this work possible. Among them a special thanks to Jan, Sophie, Bob M., Peter R., Michael, my children Ahven and Fergus, my dad, and my mother who is long gone but always with me. Thanks to Keith at Brick Road Poetry Press, Gribble Press, and Finishing Line Press for taking a chance on me. A special thanks to Peter Wadsworth at Annalese Press for his endless belief in the quality of these poems and willingness to publish this collection along with a companion book of poems ntitled *Blue Halo*.

And finally my appreciation goes to my brother who I miss deeply and who touched my life in indelible ways.

"There are desires to return, to love, to not disappear,
and there are desires to die, fought by two
opposing waters that have never isthmused."

Cesar Vallejo

# Contents

## Part One  *Blue Pantomime*

| | |
|---|---|
| I am amputating | 1 |
| I know you want me to speak straight | 2 |
| You can give my brother a bucket of kisses | 4 |
| My brother is weeping | 5 |
| I tell you there was goodness in his limbs | 7 |
| My brother parades his backside | 9 |
| In the calendar pinup | 10 |
| You can eat from my brother's plate | 12 |
| In the big mall | 13 |

## Part Two  *Ace Raider*

| | |
|---|---|
| When they cut the umbilical cord | 15 |
| It is the summer of moth wings | 17 |
| When we started to grow big | 19 |
| My brother is ace raider | 20 |
| My brother rides God on a carousel | 21 |
| My father slaps you | 22 |
| My mother anchors her voice | 23 |

## Part Three  *Chicken Shit*

| | |
|---|---|
| My brother can drink a gallon of milk | 24 |
| My brother is knee deep in chicken shit | 26 |
| My brother eats salami | 28 |
| My father is angry | 32 |
| My brother tells me | 35 |
| The woman who winds her finger | 37 |
| Underneath the calm of my brother | 40 |
| The night my dad needs to hear live jazz | 41 |
| The lover who has bitten my brother's neck | 44 |
| My brother tempts fate | 45 |
| My brother can pole vault the dark | 47 |
| My brother is five parts sugar | 49 |
| My brother lives seven blocks | 50 |
| My brother doesn't pulverize his past | 51 |
| My brother gift wraps his love | 52 |
| My brother is stuck in mud | 54 |

## Part Four  *Sisyphus Hauling*

| | |
|---|---|
| My brother has a tattoo on his arm | 56 |
| My brother kept the picture | 57 |
| On his better days my brother dreams | 58 |
| My brother doesn't worship the moon | 60 |
| In the dead blue of my eyes | 61 |
| My brother soft shoes his way | 63 |
| My brother has borrowed a rifle | 64 |

## Part Five  *A Pallbearer of Adversity*

| | |
|---|---|
| My brother high stakes his cards | 66 |
| My brother is a pallbearer of adversity | 67 |
| My brother is on the bandwagon | 68 |
| In the speaker's cruise book | 69 |
| My brother wears the only pair of jeans | 71 |
| My father will probably never know | 73 |
| We are damp | 74 |

## Part Six  *St Lucia*

| | |
|---|---|
| The forensic light at the end of the world | 76 |
| My brother examines the preacher | 79 |
| My brother's courage | 80 |
| My brother is staying in St. Lucia | 81 |
| Azalea | 82 |

## Postscript

Letter to My Brother

# When you told me you wanted

to go back to her
our mother who died too young
said *she is waiting for me, don't try to interfere
know this is what I want
I'm tired sister*

in my heart of hearts I knew already
I had lost you
that you were on your way home

but I couldn't let you go yet
talked with you on the phone for over an hour
in an anonymous car park
cried, implored
till finally you gave us your motel address
on the pretext of a final farewell

and on that day, at that hour
a hand longer than my own
seemed to save you

and I told you - whatever happens
someday I am going to write a book of your life
and you said *if you ever do, tell it straight*

and so brother, who has taken the flowers
from the right ventricle of my heart
as  promised

this book is for you
and I will tell about it.

# Part One

*Blue Pantomime*

# I am amputating

my brother's hospital bracelet
its perforated blue
dull as death.

How many years have I forecast this fate
wrapped my arms around it
steeled myself for the loss?

In January the Northwest stumbles
through grey winter
blankets a leery eye
relents only long enough
for the sun to wash.

A seminary of roses
casket that will go up in flame
the way death feels
hands folded over his chest
almost peaceful.

*Don't worry for me* my brother said
six months earlier
*when I die I'm going back to her*
certain like in the early years
she would be there
look after him.

And he did.
And she does.

# I know you want me to speak straight

not romanticize the blood clots
limp from the motorcycle accident
pizza, tatter tots, gallons of milk
whistle that keeps toot toot tooting
the way you hide from people
avoid sitting in restaurants
boast a heart tattoo
across from a death skull.

I know you want me to speak straight
about the sixteen year old who paints his room black
buys friends with pot smoke
refuses to accept the world as a shop mall
wrestles my father's voice from its dustpan
makes my car run
squeezes the rain into a jar
whistles the Wizard of Oz, calms dogs
offers up surprise wisdom
when my relationships fail.

I know you want me to speak straight
about the way your body leans
works hard as a pack horse
how you are loved by bosses
have a penchant for justice
storyteller's way of poking at pretense
will never marry, raise kids
know a lover so truant
your chest outlaws ordinary joyrides.

Sometimes they say *ignorance is bliss*
but that has not been your road.
You keep up with the news, world affairs

give me history lessons, tape poignant videos
about elephants, vanishing wolves.

You are not just some drug dealer's high rise
the work till you drop employee
the seven year old kid rigging yard ramps
free spirit who early on gets caught.
You are uncle to my daughter and son
housemate and soulmate to Marion
my father's one son
my lost mother's boy child
the loyal worker
lasting soulmate to Yvonne

you are my brother
and I have loved you fiercely
will always weep over the way
you can't outrun our boxes
bait death
like me, will have trouble
figuring out how to swim here.

## You can give my brother a bucket of kisses

coo words
a slippery elm swing, sewn monkey
but you'll still never get to marry him

he is hard wired
after the angular words, insults
my father's tar pitch

hides his shrapneled heart
inside a nickelodeon
chrome wheels
inside factory flawless
steel shanked boots.

You can offer my brother
summer's yellow roses
a candlelight dinner at the coast
still not woe him.

He rigs his room with Batmobiles
an eight foot mannequin
that gobbles clothe bats, the stuffed pooch
turns a green face
wards off regular people
won't let anybody else
get close.

## My brother is weeping

as if crushed ice has its own
blue pantomime
dilapidated pony
stories to tell
not just about sick livered sunset
but  pomegranates
the Florida everglades
a Wisconsin snowfield
the rain in Hoquiam

about day laborers and pool halls
grunion summers that take more sweat
than they give
about elk meat, bagged antelope
the hunter sells in the blue café

about the man who set off with snowshoes
into the Eagle Cap Wilderness
lasted three days

about white powder
boy hurt the size of an ocean
the father who can't exorcise his hailstorms
kerosenes yard beetles
and the mother who dies young
in her blue kimono
leaves us to wander

the tall buildings, cell phones
grid work

how small we can feel
when everything can manage
so neatly
without us.

My brother is a datebook with destiny
a hosanna in the making
a cowboy in work boots
doesn't want his heart thumping
its panicked drum
to be the frenzied fire eater

doesn't want to go up in smoke
have his life cease
offer up no bread baskets
   doesn't  does  doesn't  does

but it will
it will
and try as he may to be strong
carry on here
he can't.

> I tell you there was goodness in his limbs
> the world incarnate

If he was a good boy
what does it mean
that his hair choired yellow
he kept a tidy yard, washed dishes
said please, thank you
rescued birds
took out the trash
wrote with careful penmanship
paint brushed the past
rattled love till it was not just
a thin post?

If we say he was decent
what does that mean
he said his prayers
ate fish on Friday
knew the Hail Mary
words that mean mercy
knew more than words
their beginning and ends
could curly cue sunsets
parapet the dark
nurse crocus
knew that we sleep in a fetal pressed nest egg
are no one's bandied day mill

does it mean he strove hard
set up a durable cook set
mapped time well
put it to order with a schoolboy's diligence

the double breasted blazer, combed shoes
night's hymnal
set to right his subtraction tables

does it mean he married brightly
claimed a big house, expensive armchairs
dusted words
perpetually greened his grass
moved flawless

loved his job, stock
his family, life
refused to pilfer
break bones
expatriate his heart

flapped like a reliable duck
for our breadcrumbs
the seat fit
he drove and drove
suction cupped the night to speak easy

does it mean he hooked lust
to the end of a tailgate
a stranger's home
drug deal
his past
my mother's loose leaf

traveled to any place good boys go
on a thin July day
while calculated summer
hangs pert on a billboard?

## My brother parades his backside

for no one but him.
Who will find him lovely
lessen the blows, the pipes, the foil
the load on his back daily
the callouses of his work hands
if you do not

who will call his name, its almost invisible
call it true and clean and eager
listen to his jokes, politics
his resignation over our inhumanity
if you are missing

who will mind the cough
offer up more than blue pills
the grave he is digging
if you do not

find him beautiful
worthy to be cared for
to the last?

## In the calendar pinup

my brother's body is missing
will never show up
is just a scissored page
disavowed mass that grew big
worried that fat is a fate of death
in a slim fast world.

My brother was uncomfortable
in restaurants, gyms
avoided holiday parties
was determined to be thin
not let any drug pusher scratch holes
starved himself as if denial saves.

Come evening, his body depleted
from dragging hoses all over the city
he'd exercise on the recumbent bike
and I'd watch the sweat pour off his chin
hold in my secret weeping.
Later he'd fry hot dogs, heat pizza
slump in the armchair
call what was on his tray *a good meal*.

My brother made me laugh
recited endless news stories
had a high I.Q., was able to debate
held a tough line when it comes to
human values of decency, work ethic
yet was too shy to go to a dance hall
attend a wedding reception
turn up at a beach condo.

My brother had hair the color of velocity
eyes so blue the sea found its mirror
will never know a wife
family, home
worked his ass off
at jobs nobody else that smart
wants to do
took tons of overtime
was hardly ever sick
didn't manage to spend his vacations
spread a blanket at the beach
had half his pay withheld
for some poor man's retirement cabin.

The sharp writing my brother penned
about the 26 states he lived in
the crazy antics, antidotes
will never reach a press
be a bound book, New York Times bestseller
will die the anonymity our world lends.

Not all things come to glory.
Not all of us are the palliative of silver spoons
college degrees, ride tickets.
Some of us bust ass and get lost
are the bored kid in the classroom
the never good enough child
the dead mother's favorite
are deemed almost forgettable
go down on our knees
don't know how to get back up
navigate the losses
need somebody to be there.
Not all things come to glory here.

## You can eat from my brother's plate

witness the scant of it
its no nonsense ball park franks, brave militia
its mustard and metal turnstiles
its scrimshaw blades, potato salad
family of charge cards

you can pick through my brother's room
witness the lean and dark of it
its wax museum figures, fake Rambo blade
its travelogue of neat tees
bent hope, expensive cologne
arrested side mirrors.

You can populate my brother's thoughts
worry about the wrought iron of them
their rifled rooms, war zones
limp forsythia
their BB guns, baby boy blue wheels.

You can map my brother's hands
travel the prolonged size of them
smell the emptied grease traps
26 states, lack of cruise liners
their cramped roads, mechanical wizardry
their grunt moans, day labor
their rest in peace  rest in peace
final nesting.

You can talk to my brother's heart
listen to the sighs of it
its genuine and malt coated
wire cages, animal kingdoms
its button up    button up
all gone in the cold.

# In the big mall

my brother does not stand out
not even his 6'3" looks formidable
he is dressed in ordinary jeans
a maroon tee, sneakers
uneasy with crowds, his thick body
the possibility others judge
will shrink into the sideline
of vinyl seats.

My brother can impersonate Boris Karloff
The Three Stooges, Buzz Lightyear
fan a deck of cards, pick out the queen
draw rabbits from a black topper
perfect grill ballpark franks
set off fireworks, sticks of dynamite
has a wicked sense of humor
which many others do not.

My brother's death may seem diminutive
a quarter column in the newspaper
a funeral service with thirty folks

may seem as small as a side alley
leftover pizza
the shy man who walks with a limp
in a big mall

but if you think this way
you will miss something
the ruby in the pea

the way dim surfaces
hold colored light

how a voice sounds when it's noticed
not withered on the vine
but unpeeled

that what we truly witness
saves.

# Part Two

*Ace Raider*

## When they cut the umbilical chord

wrap my brother's premature body in the plaid blanket
and my mother nurses him careful
I am already five years old.
When the hospitalizations, bouts of croup
nearly claim
she pronounces him *delicate*
a tender pup in a sea of tar paper
permissions him only later to be a daredevil.

My brother wades in the blue of my mother's eyes
splashes her ankles
gobbles her cake
cools off inside her summer kisses
never tires of the sea she provides
will dig up yard grass
plant wood ramps over the iris
to fly toward the sun

later breaks an arm, his leg
tugs on the Christmas tree till it falls
places his curious finger in the whirring blade
of the box fan
plays sleuth to prove
there is no Santa.

My mother humors him with ice cream
takeout pizza when he's too shy to sit in restaurants
go to summer camp, family gatherings
calls him from work
worries my father will act out
shoot his mouth off in blue daggers
then offer up sausage

worries she's not there
my brother's life will ink black
consoles him with éclairs, new jeans
a portable stereo
grilled hot dogs, corned beef hash.

My brother hovers between the prize peacock
and being damned
between two standards of decency
the father who swims raucous beetles in kerosene
a mother who offers up spandex
a boundless sea
orange life jackets.

When my brother paints his walls black
as a bat cave, pot smokes his nights
locks himself in
some of us look the other way.
Is he really misunderstood, troubled?
*A punk* in my father's words
or a wounded boy in a six foot three body
about to enter a life's worth
of rollercoasters?

## It is the summer of moth wings

clothes drying on the line
flying beasties
a blue rubber pool in Mary Lou's backyard.
The street sweepers have hosed the roads
our mothers look pretty
their red lipstick, tight cut petal pushers.
I have grown two inches in five months
my shorts barely zip.

My brother makes our father irritable
rigs ramps in the yard
wants to jump flame
become more than incidental.

I spy a ship with my binoculars
pebble beach
palm trees, blue island.

It is the summer of a Queens heatwave
box fans sold out at every store
our bodies chained to a park sprinkler
Mary Lou pool dates
snow cones
the boat basin at Jones Beach
sharks that don't bite
feed on small fingers
flippered feet

the world still swims
in treacle water.

My brother will grow up to be six foot
like my father

dream a world out of my mother's ashes
hug trees
eat pizza
tell us his stupid jokes
test his finger in a fan blade
will never marry
have kids
own a house.

It is the summer of moth wings
bicycle horns, running bases
Mr. Bungalow Bar up the street

we think our youth will last
that my brother will always
look for the rise of a high note
drum the table with his spoons
coo so close to my mother
the birds grow jealous

call himself the *Mad Rider of the Northern Sky*
make it stick.

With his revved up mini bike, daredevil jumps
indomitable eye of the sun on his tee shirt
nobody expects my brother to depart the earth
except as an astronaut

nobody expects the crushed lack of magnificence
his pale frame, curled body
dead

as if in his greed
god claims him.

# When we started to grow big

our mother became fretful
not just about size
but the way the world sometimes offends
stabs oranges, offers up crème ices
then a snap turtle

was afraid of the rancor of schoolrooms
sunrise coated with menthol
the class system of roses
nursery rhymes trained to deconstruct.

When we started to grow big
mother bronzed our shoes
daisy rings
fingerprinted our toes for posterity
planted in our palm toy birds
a village of midget beach bungalows
that live past sooty.

At night after the gravied meatballs
she'd coax us into the yard
finger paint the past into a wedge of ocean
emerald dress, makeshift boat
set us to sail under a Cretian moon
till we never needed to land anywhere.

Over time we have learned to befriend water
fish with our hands
whistle the stars out of hiding
hold death in its dice roll
sing *Carolina on my mind*
into the night's damp bed.

## My brother is ace raider

of the unfathomable universe.
You don't want to mess with him
call him guerilla when his back is turned
pussyfoot your words as if his brain's gone missing.

He eats fire, rubble, pine cones
spins on a blue axis
will fix your brakes
overhaul your engine
trip wire the past
till it speaks no dirty.

My brother is ace raider
of the unfathomable universe
spills card tricks, pink rabbits
out of a felt hat
codifies the Danube

clears the money laundering
self-satisfied, speed traps.

See the way he manhandles his wheels
slurs past trees, blue crane, skyscrapers
sucks up the scenery
full throttle
goes for broke
till the crash.

## My brother rides God on a carousel

goes up and down the brass rod
of his brown pony
the one with the coarse mane
knotted thread

rides as if death
will wait
tugs at the reins
shouts *faster, faster*
kicks

grabs for the gold ring
promise of a stuffed bear
free ride tickets.

My brother wants the chance to climb
a bigger stead
mount the black one with the gold bridle
go for a second time
a third
a fourth.

On the park bench
my mother watches
waves.

## My father slaps you

claims somebody has to knock in some sense
doesn't deal with backtalk, believe you
can score a good report card, fix the sink
on this day are anything but *a punk*.

Two days from now he will shout to you
about the Patriots, their winning streak
knows they're your favorite team
will ask if you want chorizo, fries
as if nothing bad ever happens

as if the two of you are best buddies
about to share onion dip, chips, sausage
spread out in the living room
compare scores
cheer for your opposite team.

# My mother anchors her voice

to the sparrows
learns to chirp
perk up iris
dry mud
bird coo my father's insolence

keeps her best voice for last
the disordered speech of her night dreams
walks out in a slinky robe
drops it by the side of the pool
goes in naked.

Even the purple glow of the pool's aqua lights
barely hint at the heft of her nipples
the rhythm of her breast stroke
the way her accursed life

by nightfall
turns lithe as a selkie.

# Part Three

*Chicken Shit*

# My brother can drink a gallon of milk

finish off a Sicilian pizza
when the night grows threadbare
and his height shifts
can hoist up the car
sweet talk a willing lady
smash ping pong balls
preface Armageddon.

He has no patience for falsehood
people who spin shiny lures
polish hub caps
disguise a sludge pond.

My brother tells stories that can wet our pants
propagate weeping.
They are wedded to world news
work hijinks, catastrophes
bomb defuses, crime cases
he follows with a rapt curiosity.
*Let me tell you this one* he'll say
and go on about the monkey in Algeria
stuck in some metal trap elevator
that goes berserk with two kids
or the clock repair man who hides
a two karat South African diamond
worth $750,000 inside the fine precision
of a pocket watch bound for Switzerland
escapes Nazi detention with a nest egg.

I ask him about weather patterns
next week's forecast, if the stock market
will collapse, if the fanatics hoarding

two years of rations in underground bunkers
know something I can't see.

My brother has an encyclopedic version
of the world in his wings.
Diagnostics.
Claims not every place in America
is a Hollywood set, inscrutable.
Keeps Italian knives, unworn gold watches
boxed Tour de France sunglasses
a wicked witch of the west in his room
that turns green in the face.
She has swallowed Dorothy's dog
clearly does sinister things
without asking.

# My brother is knee deep in chicken shit

but it's his yard
and I'm not saying.

He has a habit of letting fly
what he loves
making a lopsided kingdom
some cardboard version of scenery.

But it doesn't work.
The upholstery upends.
The shoe box grows tight.
The girl revolts.
Kids disappear into childcare
a fabricated universe.

The monkey lady impregnates his heart
offers up calypso orchids in winter
covers over her black as sin in an eyelet dress
to tamper with her is to be confronted
by invisible knife wounds.

My brother is knee deep in chicken shit
since he hen housed his backyard
won't listen to sweet talk
fumes over conservative politics on the radio
the way the boss cuts their life insurance
employee health care
how the songbird won't sing.

My brother is knee deep in chicken shit
tells me the nights get lonely
his heart fights to reach out of his chest

pound down a fence
he can't sleep because of the cough

worries that for months
no one has diagnosed this
as anything more than the minor
inconvenience of acid reflex
heartburn.

# My brother eats salami

wonders where the day goes.
It is 4pm and he needs to be in bed by 7
since his job starts in the middle of the night
and he just jump-started my car
tells me *be sure to check your antifreeze*

observes his route is too big
his boss slums in Boca Raton
after wedding the new wife
the epic facelift,
that the restaurant oil is so thick from the cold
you need to torch gun it to get it to flow,
that at the state penitentiary this week
he spent an hour cracking jokes with the prison guards
before the oil was loose enough to lift,
claims the women *aren't half bad*,
warns me of certain restaurants where the oil
is so gelled, clouded over *you don't want to eat there*
and I start rethinking my food habits.
I've seen him at the end of the day with his heavy boots
overalls covered with sludge
anxious to get home to a shower, lazy boy recliner, pizza
some poor man's dream of a compact cabin
in the woods.

In the cold damp of a Northwest winter
you can think many things about life.
That it's a hipster's paradise
that gourmet coconut kiwi crème donuts
are a hot item
that when traveling on mountain roads to ski
bring chains
about the excellent and the deplorable

the way the women prisoners move
how many attempts it takes to mouth organ the moon
what it siphons out of your hide to work 50, 70 hours
be a pack mule that raises up others' tanned lives

in the cold damp of a Portland winter
you can start to doubt yourself
the tried and truisms
the pledge to a flag you recited daily
with your hand over your heart
your scout pins, pool trophies
Eagle songs and Motown

start to doubt how the American work ethic tastes
how public money gets spent
whether your niece and nephew will have a decent planet
handed down to them.

My brother is about to drive home
slouch in the recliner, kick up his feet, watch the news
learn about rapes, rugby, a Mars mission
eat his pizza, then doze off to sleep in his body
that is tall and stocky as a longshoreman
has been a cat driver, worked rock quarries
lifted house furniture, managed apartment maintenance
been a garbage collector, and now hauls
heavy hoses into restaurant kitchens
sucks up their grease
loads it in his truck and drives miles through traffic
over his city route
to turn sludge into biodiesel.

If you think he is a simple man
slow on the uptake, a gobbler of Kung Fu movies
backyard beer parties
you'd be wrong.

He shoots the breeze with the Asian restaurant owners,
the kitchen help at the Oyster Bar in the Pearl
the prison guards
tells me of the politics they talk
how it screws with your head in solitary confinement
the way the Golden Triangle owners on 5th are cutting down
on their menu, use their teenage daughter and son to wait tables
how the red eyed Polish vendor lost his food license
has just staked up a sign *tables for five bucks apiece*
tells me about cockroaches and what shows up in a trash bin
how his co-workers bust their ass
while their health premium goes up
tells me there's no place for a poor man
in the sea of America
but I don't want to believe this.

My brother busts his ass
makes his pay by doing 50 plus hour weeks.
For years has driven old cars, doesn't own a house
decent stereo, futon bed, collection of nice furniture
swing set for imaginary kids
with the limp and the pins in his leg
will never climb a mountain, snowshoe, ride a bike.
He comes home coated with filth
showers, scours his hands with a thick wire brush
chemical liquid.

It is February. The oil is hard as old fashioned Crisco.
The blow torch is slow but works.
He will limp his way in and out of the back alley
of the restaurants, drag the heavy hoses
avoid rats, things too offensive to mention
that have to do with sanitation, cutting corners
staying afloat, making our food.

He will die one week before his 50th birthday
and I can't help but wonder
will the restaurant owners, the prison guards
the takeout pizza delivery boy
the company owner tanned and newly youthful
with his pert wife, second and third homes
his maxed out co-workers
will any of them remember him?

## My father is angry

as if god stomps and nobody cares
86-years-old he complains about this and that
swears the recessed light wasn't fixed right
complains about the doctor's appointment
how the world keeps bleeding him
the bus driver never sticks to his timetable
everything goes wrong.

If you and I were to calculate his
in love with life ratio
it would depend on the day
the succulence of the meat roasting
the rude ring of the phone
the level of flame inside the
ruse of the field's burning.

I have lived years under his spell.
We could chalk it up to old age
my brother's recent death
the way the old get marginalized
or what it's like to have your mother die
while you're still in a crib
be sent away to an orphanage
grow up with an alcoholic dad
who refuses to let you get adopted
later turns a blind eye when his girlfriend rapes you
forces you to move school twelve times
abandon your boyhood treasures to storage lockers

we could chalk it up to a world with crushed ice
too many bee stings, a no bicycle past
a bureaucracy that buries your dining table
in junk mail, medical bills, charity requests

we could ask my mother
that Liz Taylor look-a-like turned
late night purveyor of ice cream
ask her to consult some outjie board
ignore the years of accusations crammed down her throat
the angry tirades, whether it was about giblets
in the gravy, or the way children don't listen
secretly plot to spit in your face
the crushed boyhood blue of his heart flailing.

My father has a frozen view of the world
secretly sees life as thorn ridden
says *dreams are a luxury I learned I'd never have*
never forgets to refill his birdfeeders
likes to cut me down to size
sharpen his knife blade
the next day won't remember
will hand me a bag of red peppers
barley soup, bunch of scallions
he's hauled from the store.

My father is from the Bronx
has worked hard all his life
has a high I.Q.
stays up late night, reads the newspapers
checks out facts on the computer
Tweets about ball games, Nina Simone
has buried two wives and my brother.
I am the only one left for him.

He notices the cherry blossoms come April
serenades the lilac, peonies
speaks to strangers as if he is the world's
best lottery winner
swears by his Yankees baseball
loves shrimp, fried rice, German pastries

new restaurants
remembers back streets in Paris, Montserrat
his favorite fish joint in San Francisco
buys Tillamook huckleberry ice cream

takes two buses to play pinochle three days a week
goes to hear klezmer music, good jazz

can switch on a dime
call me worthless
become the destroyer of June bugs
dump their invasive bodies
into his coffee tin
laced with kerosene
watch them squirm.

## My brother tells me

our father calls every night
wants to talk
says it drives him crazy
but he can't say *no*
holds the receiver a mile away from his head.
My father doesn't try it with me
probably because I have two kids and campus
says *you are always making excuses you are too busy*
as if I lie.

My father has no conscience about what he asks
what others have going
expects he and my brother will buy a condo
live together come April.

Two years ago my dad never knew the truth about
why my brother couldn't make his paid flight
to the East Coast to drive him across country
once the moving truck was sent off with his stuff.
I covered, said *Chris is sick in the hospital*
not the sad truth that my brother went off
on a drug binge after months of not using
ended up in the emergency room with serious chest pain
couldn't face the drive across country
seven to ten planned days, 24 hours a day
alone in the car with my dad.
This is what a past
the scars we hold
can do to someone.

Is it a coincidence I worked my tail off
in school for good grades

a perfect report card
tried to win some approval I never got
then made myself pencil thin
after college never came home to visit my father
without a man by my side
someone who could protect me
fend off the barbs
keep his words, his anger at arm's length.

And as a child I still remember come spring
the lilacs my father picked
delivered to my room in a bud vase
as if my mother wasn't whittling to death
under his blue razors
as if the house sang in a May breeze

and I wonder about the things we erase
try to forget
the pins and needles, arsenic we impose on a heart
the way the mind works
my father's orphaned childhood, abused past
the way he laughs with the neighbors
admires other people's kids
tyrants my mother's heart
stomps on us then offers up cheesecake

how sometimes the past comes back
to taunt
big as a stick.

# The woman who winds her finger

around you
gives you the more and more and more
that plagiarizes your heart

claims her daughter and son have to be returned
to their dad in Vancouver by 9am
a couple of hours but she will take the bus
doesn't want to trouble anyone
the one who gives you the sob story
chokes your already mangled heart
till you give her your car keys
credit card, cash
*for gas, just in case*

never travels back to you
sprawled out, fried in the airport motel room.
And maybe, come morning
in the blurry that is ordinary
it is easy to feel everybody has their scheme
sharp angle
that if you are just one time gullible
you'll be left a chump in cheap jeans.

Some people phantom the dark
with motorcycles
the life that once was
might be
the father who reminds
*you have never amounted to anything.*

The woman in the motel room
with her guy friends
borrows your car

your credit card, goodwill
elopes with something more
never looks back.

Deserted next morning, your charge card
jacked up $20,000, car gone
your life in another one of its shambles
you say *somebody is going to pay*
phone the police, report burglary
fan the Italian stiletto you've
unpacked from the cardboard box.

Back home, in the middle of three nights
two guys come and bang at the front door
shout obscenities
how they are going to whip you for reporting
the stolen car, credit card.

Your housemate pops sedatives, sleeping pills
is afraid, doesn't want these guys to know where you live
worries you stay up late, wait on a serrated edge
have borrowed a 45
prop it by the side of the television
lay five knifes face up on a tray table.
Desperation, has many faces
as if an eye for an eye for an eye
will get us some place.

You phone me
*I've got to be honest with you
our lives are in grave danger
these guys are going to work hard
to get back at me.*
I am afraid.

What will happen weeks from now
when your willpower fails
when the whistle man toots
with his white cake powder claims of paradise
where will you go
who will look after you
why do they shout their obscenities
threaten to break your legs

who will be left
at the end of the day
crouched in the shadows waiting?

# Underneath the calm of my brother

a compulsive city burns.
He knows life can chew chiffon
gobble what it takes
that injustice gets dismissed as chew candy
the blind leading the blind
*and why the hell have they cut our health
benefits anyway?*

My brother has a calm that is born
of street malls
poorboy sandwiches
the black eye my father gave him
years ago when he wasn't listening.

You don't want to mess with
his boyhood fantasies
his guerrilla warfare, stacks of dynamite
collection of Italian stilettos
the fake Rambo with its big blade.

My brother could cash in
on the seventh life he is living
be gone in a flash
like the firecrackers he sets off
the dangerous ones
in the name of thrill seeking.

He will stop at ATM machines
go a long way down the road
to get that extra thrill
the monkey lady happily provides
in the motel where she sells to him.

## The night my dad needs to hear live jazz

even though there is only an hour left
and you, my maybe British boyfriend
drive the snare of one way streets
that circumvent the historic train district
while I grow impatient over how time is tight
want you to have a seismic set of maps
in your head

the night we finally sit at the table
catch the last session of the vocalist
and my dad orders oysters but doesn't like the sauce
and with joy you gobble up the rest on his plate
finish the bread pudding he claims is almost magnificent
except for the raisins

the night I catch a side glance of you at the three top table
your long silvered hair, the way our eyes meet and pause
two ships that honor each other in a rankless sea

the night we leave happy, a talented cello player
the vocalist from Denmark, attentive chef to my dad
and we go back to the parking lot beneath the overpass
where my old vehicle waits
and my brother rings
wants *to say goodbye*, won't tell me where he is
wants to die in an anonymous motel room
tells me he's *going back to her*

the night I cry and plead for over an hour in the back seat
plead for him to not go
while he says *it's time, I am tired*
even though he is in his forties
claims our mother waits

and I plead more
*you need to at least give me an address*
*to say one last goodbye*
and my brother hedges, and my dad wants the phone
wants to knock in some sense
but my brother says *no*

and then I give the phone to you
some British stranger he has never met
boyfriend he's heard about
and somehow after a while with your gentle voice
you manage to get the address on S.E. 82nd
but my brother says he will only let you up
only open the door for you
and we speed across town
and you go up into the room, #11
where my brother says he has taken such an overdose of crack
no ordinary person can live through it
and he's been having massive heart seizures
and you pray with him
pray with him
pray with him

then he lets me up
and I am afraid
his slurred words, messed up state
but my brother's death this night gets diverted
and finally he lets my father come up
says *Hey, big man, did it feel good hitting me,*
*forcing me to fight other kids in the yard?*
and my father looks at him smugly and says *you deserved it,*
*somebody had to knock sense into you*
and my brother almost wails on my dad
but resists, and you calm things down
till my father goes back down to the car

and my brother relents, cleans up his stuff in the motel room
feels he needs to make up to the old man, 86years old
man who has criticized him merciless
yet loves him sharp as a knife blade

says *I need to apologize, make things good*
*will have dad sleep over tonight at my place*
as if nothing out of the ordinary has happened
no painful words were uttered
by a small boy with a truncated heart
and after the cleanup
getting them up the road, father and son
shaky but in one piece
I pause and wonder about who you are.

Tonight, the first time you meet my brother
under the hardest of circumstances
you move past the swear words
his garbled speech
tough guy indignities
tell me simply –
*He is a good man underneath.  We prayed together.*
*I think it may have helped.*

# The lover who has bitten my brother's neck

sears his body
is not silkier than the moon
not merciful
will not cradle him in a hard rain
talc his body
whisper coo words
after the lovemaking
scramble eggs.

The lover who has bitten my brother's neck
culls his words
draws blood
will not mother him
protect him from floods
avalanche
himself
will not vouchsafe to be friendly
stay close when the money runs out.
Things after all are provisional.

The lover who has bitten my brother's neck
will call twenty four seven
promise to never leave
never leave
tell him he is blameless
can defy gravity
shoot a bull's-eye
unlike my dad
never need to be alone
act perfect.

## My brother tempts fate

with drug dealers who would
just as soon break his arm
torch the townhouse
then go without the money owed
as if a pawn shop can save him
fancy Seiko watches
Oakley sunglasses
bribes and trades and
*get me what I need bro.*

And if the free basing is killing you
the sex life is nonexistent
and your boss lauds you for your industry
and pack animal
to slug your body in the middle of the night
coated in restaurant grease
haul ass in the big truck
with the gutless hoses

maybe it's just life
the big "I" of it
how it eats up what it chucks
can crush a busted boy
play Russian roulette
terrorize a townhouse
threaten to break every bone.

But then living on the edge between danger
and death has that kind of exuberance

the gold bracelets and crack, late night munchies
baited fate
feeding it frill words and honey
the way matadors tempt bulls
stuntmen spit at death

after all, who'd want to mess with you
and who'd want to fake heart failure
clean up a motel room pretty
have you lying there neat as an
unsullied businessman
a soda by the bed
the sheets carefully turned down.

See how a death can be orchestrated
till somebody anonymous disappears
see what your sister will and will not learn
from the medical examiner's report

see what I will make of your monkey lady
her two kids, the bags she pushes
whose life is a *fucking no mercy*
*kill them as you go*
see what I will make of those vendettas
that middle of the night screw turning
the golden greed of their armpits.

## My brother can pole vault the dark

but he has to be willing

like the preacher says
at the N.A. meetings
and the higher power that takes your shit
and turns it into a halo
and the ATM machine says

and the dark lady who wants
lego money for her two kids
and a house at the coast

who can't afford to worry
about his chest pain
or enough is enough is enough

when there is never enough
and after all, we *are* willing
and money speaks, doesn't it.

My brother can pole vault the dark
croupier the moon
if he is able to break from this

set up a leper colony
missionary outpost

walk the sand
see his hard-won job money

turn into a prevention program
cabin in Wisconsin
fishing trip
best selling book
beach vacation in St. Lucia.

## My brother is five parts sugar

and a sea of mud
won't last
the migratory and the attrition
the way he wears out the habitual
the ordinary peril of things
my father's whiplash

dreams a dead mother
50,000 ways to come clean
be a forensic expert, bomb diffuser.

My brother mines the day
of its broken scenery
sucks up restaurant oil
hauls ass hard as a worker bee
shoots the breeze with
the cook at the Ming Garden
vendors of tacos, tamales, spring rolls, gyros
with ladies who execute a powder perfect face job
makes them laugh, commiserate about Iraq, the economy
the waiter with cancer, no health care
the displaced millworkers, shellshock future
can divert attention from the holes we are sleeping in
that dissonance that grows heavier than a bank vault.

My brother is a 2 x 4, a seven year old boy
on a souped up bike, trilogy of yard jumps, firecrackers
can't manage to eat in a restaurant on his time off
won't ever marry, raise kids
set foot in a gym
look at himself close in the dark.

In my brother a shitload of our
broken mirrors are floating.

## My brother lives seven blocks

from the mall
but won't shop there
orders online
hopes the tee shirts fit
the socks, in packs of twelve
live up to their price.

At 6'3" he doesn't fit into everything.
Collects Seiko watches, fancy sunglasses
offers them down the road for trade
knows time may be catching up
with the stabs in his chest.

My brother can swear on a dime
and win a bet with his hands closed
but won't win at life
as if the cards are stacked
like the three expensive treatment programs
that I have no polite words to describe
but this is America
when it comes to health service
everything is a business and up for grabs.

My brother has never stolen
punched a cop
set a mattress on fire
works fifty hours a week
doing jobs most of us refuse to consider
is conscientious
loved by his bosses as a dedicated worker
never wants to be viewed as delinquent
will keep the mercy in his blue eyes right up
till that one fateful night in a motel room.

## My brother doesn't pulverize his past

just eats it
smokes it
snorts it
jams it down his throat
red hot coals and camphor

but in the dent of his blue blue eyes
the sea of Galilee keeps calling

amid the hub caps, and 26 states
and starting over
and $20 in his pocket
and the good looks and lonely nights
and hallucinatory day jobs coated in grease

amid the sweated brow, frozen pizzas
the gone for gold treatment centers
the *start agains*
the no insurance $32,000 back surgery
the crippled knee
crippled past    crippled past

the Sea of Galilee in the liquid ardor
of my brother's blue blue eyes
keeps calling.

# My brother gift wraps his love

is the generous uncle
man with a wicked sense of humor
who carries a hand grenade in his throat.
Nobody is saying.
Some things are so painful
we wall them into paper planes
all-season tires, a gutless phone
want to believe in the cabin in Wisconsin
some poor guy's retirement dream

want to believe that luck finally saves
with its rustproof rails, sense of grace
want to believe there are no pins in his leg
no more haul ass jobs
sweated brow, endless overtime
the never get ahead
never get ahead
before the monkey lady claims.

She has two kids, on the surface manages a motel
along a stretch of strip joints, 24 hour coffee
doesn't muddle her brain
worry about the periled hearts she fries
bags the stuff like candy
colored April.
Part of me says – *for shame on you*
for shame the way you make a living
breed death as if it is only fountain pens.
Part of me says - *may you die*
*with rats in your grave*
for the years of life my brother will never know.

My father says we are what we make
that nobody twists our arm
and an ounce of willpower is worth more
than those three useless $15,000 plus
treatment programs
the ones I visited that felt more like anonymous street malls.
Does my father keep an airtight version
of heroism in his head, success by bootstraps

an uncorrupt place where everybody sleeps decent
enjoys hand-blown scenery
place where even an orphaned child
can grow to be a man without drink
steady bill payer
as if stamina saves us, *just say no*
is written across every billboard along with the
ads for beer, cocktails, beauty, casinos.

# My brother is stuck in mud

that won't vaporize.
I send him a spotty the dog
hand size red convertible
timetable for love

but he will have none of it
just the gold Seiko watches
pro sunglasses
things you can use for a bribe
pawn around to cover a want addiction.

*Don't go there* I say
as if there is a penmanship that eludes him
untold quadrant of the city that feeds off
busted lament
caution tape.

And as for those vampires of the dark
what about them
the ones who will steal a wallet, car
bust headlights
prosper the watches
a pocket full of credit cards as if they are oatmeal
watch him get wasted
in an economy motel bed

let him beg for company
run when his heart starts fisting up
the palpitations get fierce
wear down his strong man totem

and the woman (I want to scratch
your eyes out honey)
the one with the two kids

who passes for a motel manager
dispenses pretty bags
doesn't give a shit about my brother's heart racing.
Business is business.

America – thank you for your decent
affordable treatment programs
for your no nonsense around
our dinner tables.

She will turn a stiff face
walk away along with the others
till you are alone in the wasted motel room
beg me on the phone to come over
stay vigil
drive you to the emergency room.

# Part Four

*Sisyphus Hauling*

## My brother has a tattoo on his arm

so big the skull looks distorted
the grim reaper has arrived.
The tattoo is a hazard of his teenage years
when he painted the walls black
made a god out of birthday money
Christmas money, car wash money, shoe shine
till his jars were full
and he uploaded a torched heart, dark skull
raced a motorcycle, bought a fancy truck
jacked up the wheels.

Sometimes we decide we are impervious to death
go around with our ass in its face
as if we can conquer anything
roll joints, buy it, sell it, sew it in our seams
nothing seems incorruptible
all our friends are on the same page cruising for something.

Sometimes death knows no country, no equinox, no trespass
has a will of its own
will pull a small boy through pond ice
drag us under a car, slow our body with cancer
ping pong the life we've been living
shovel dirt till the ground grows crooked
and Celeste says- *Why won't you marry me?*
and before we can figure out the answer to her
or for that matter to any other question of equal worth

the light dims, the ground calls back midnight
and every promise, hope, dream we've ever made
is a skeletal shipwreck.

## My brother kept the picture

of my mother, the two of us, in an oval frame.
There is no father, perhaps he was taking the photograph
or had gone missing
become an angry fist
invisible blade.

My brother keeps car records, New England Patriot ball caps
expensive cologne
keeps my poetry books, rubber gloves for work
in a cardboard box on the top shelf
has stopped accumulating
what can't be moved or sold.

My brother's forty plus years can fit
on a pinky finger
into a side note
blue cubby

but I know that a life is worth
more than this
more than shop malls, blue asphalt, tv soaps
more than back breaking work
more than sweet treat dealers
82$^{nd}$ Avenue motels
more than Sisyphus hauling the rock
hauling the rock
grown almost unbearable.

## On his better days my brother dreams

retirement, a plot of land
cheap rent, lots of trees
dreams the arrows of the dark
stop hurting.

On his better days my brother remembers Maine
his first girlfriend
his niece and nephew that might pass for his kids
remembers four wheelers and snowfall
back roads from Gardiner to the coast.

On his better days my brother ends
his phone calls with *love you*
the world doesn't seem inscrutable
the job orders him a new truck, decent radio
his social security one day kicks in
he sits in a restaurant unashamed
writes pen pals, plans a beach trip

there's no chronic cough
he sleeps ok when he lies down
the weight melts off easy as ice thaw.

On his better days my brother
defuses bombs, saves millions
the Iraq village is not burnt
nobody wakes to nightmares
the kitchen sink works
we have decent health care
the world is good to him
folks get by working single shifts
don't need to slaughter their body

in the name of pay
the old car is reliable
the dog waits

somewhere in the vanishing angle
of possibility
there is a patient woman
the prospect of lovemaking.

# My brother doesn't worship the moon

likes BB guns since my father
showed him how to aim and take out squirrels.
Never forgave him for forcing the fights
*bust these kids' asses before they call you a sissy.*

My brother hates my father for the
cruel words he has spilled
the never good enough, smart enough, capable
but he isn't saying.
They talk Yankees, New England Patriots
the cold snap, whether the budget will pass
as if love and hate are the double rim of a coat sleeve
go around handshaking, shoot crap with the moon
see who is going to win or lose last inning.

After hours hauling ass in his truck
my brother listens to my dad on the phone nightly
tells me *I am going crazy*
drives over to the tech store and fits
a new cord on my dad's computer
is expected to arrive on time after work Friday afternoons
take him for a good meal, movie.

My brother is squeezed in a lot of directions.
My father is convinced that come April
the two of them will buy a condo
eliminate his lonely.
My brother tells me *I can't do it, can't*
but won't say
will depart this life with alleged heart failure
in an anonymous motel room
ten days into the New Year.

## In the dead blue of my eyes

my brother stalks.
He is a chunky man
anxious and in need of sleep
slips from room to room
pours milk, warms pizza
works to keep a season of bees from stinging

tells me he's scared of the guys stalking him
scared of the cough that starts
whenever he lays down.

In the blue of my ear
I hear my brother's fetal voice
its pall mall, grainy woodwork, scutted wheels
delusory and politics
and I know he can snap a plank
pulverize anyone who hurts me
stare down a rabid dog
rescue a kid.

*Look at the moon* I say
pointing beyond the wanton sky
its muddled singsong
grey smirk that hazards
a Northwest winter

and my brother knows defiance
the *finger up your ass and shove it* routine
but someday I want to snowshoe with him
on a trail past Madras
snowshoe under a moon like this one
clear, big, vaporless.
*Look at the moon!* I say

as he microwaves one more slice of pizza
am not sure he hears,
that what I am proposing
will ever happen.
My brother has pins in his knee
disguises the limp
never walks far down the street
just works, drives our 86 year old dad.

I am his older sister, only sibling
the one he is measured by
the one he has moved across country to be near
who years ago could not save our mother
will not be able to save him.

*Look at the moon* I implore, my voice shaky
but he does not look past the dark
sponges the grease off his pizza
wonders if he'll be able to sleep
why the doctor ups his meds
dismisses the chronic cough as heartburn.

My brother has insurance, a managed care plan.
For the last three months he has gone in
talked with the doctor in his quiet way
been told the same thing – *acid reflex* – given more pills
holds no faith in what they say.

Does he already know one Friday evening
a couple of weeks from now
in a motel room on 82nd
with three guys holding their vendetta
a glass full of Pepsi by his side
his heart will fail
swim back toward my mother
and away from me?

## My brother soft shoes his way

around the apartment
doesn't want to wake anyone.
I watch him move in the shadow
drink from the rain
rotate catastrophes

relive my mother's antidotes
her gauze wings
the aeronautic way her voice sings
propagates chartreuse
holds him together
a puppet on evangelical strings
keeps the wind from wrenching.

My brother soft shoes around the grocery
as if it never turns traitor
is his best buddy
ammunition against disaster
anonymous motel rooms
is worth more than the six pack of Pepsi
devil dogs, sliced pepperoni.

My brother soft shoes around the life
he has borrowed
its snub nose and short fuse
deferred blue men
packs a borrowed rifle
waits on their night's vengeance
threats to tear down the door
erase him

will take them out one by one
with the power of indignation
that burns in him.

# My brother has borrowed a rifle

tells me *no mother fucker is going
to take me out without a fight*
smash down the front door
in the middle of the night
terrorize his housemate
make a blood bath of the carpet.

It started two weeks ago
a few days after the drug fiasco
and his stolen car, forged credit cards.
Now there is the middle of the night
thump on the front door, roulette slurs
threats of injury
the claim they will take him out
when he least expects.

And I am fearful of what drug dealers
will do when you cross their line
fearful of my brother's insolence
of what will happen a month from now
when he needs a fix, snaps his willpower
starts cruising 82$^{nd}$ with his want wheels.

Two weeks later my brother's body is found dead
in a cheap motel room.
Bed sheets neatly turned down.
The unknown woman gone.
No blue plastic cooler with his habitual Pepsi.
Just a neat glass 2/3 full by the side of the bed.
His shirt off.
All so tidy in the medical examiner's picture.
*No foul play* they tell me.
*Looks like heart failure.*

And I wonder what happened that night
who was the strange guy earlier at the townhouse
that my brother's housemate heard on the phone
wonder about the remnants of white powder she later found
the pipe he took everywhere
if it was going to be that kind of night
left behind on the living room tray table.

Later, the motel room so neat
his expensive gold watch, hoodie missing.
The story that the chambermaid came in next morning
found him alone, dead, at about 11am.
The blue coupe my father just bought him
when his other car went missing
still squat in the parking lot.

*Nice guy* the motel manager tells me
when I come to pick up the car.
*Came here sometimes, just wanted a single room
but we were nearly full so last night I gave him the big one.*

What is it I will know and never know
of the perilous happenings that night?

# Part Five

*A Pallbearer of Adversity*

# My brother high stakes his cards

makes us believe there's not much to them
feigns the poor hand

can be reckless
squander his single money card
in search of more
talks to the dealer, the cards
coaxes them toward him like a new bride
even with seven people playing.

I have seen him deadpan
about what he's been dealt
claim it is worth *less than a prairie dog*
only to fry us
grow a massive puddle of chips
when his sly hand gets played.
But he is funny as hell so
we forgive him.

Because my brother knows defeat
broken jobs, a $32,000 no insurance back surgery
knows how things in life like money, cars
slip through your fingers
he never grows morbid when he's had a bad night
seems to chalk it up to fate
a pattern his life wields
the way some people polish fancy floors
others trek work boots over plain linoleum
how there are so many ways to bring someone to mercy
come to us with a paralytic blue gaze.

## My brother is a pallbearer of adversity

squeeze him dry and he still comes back
with a song and a dance number
a puff ball of easy rhetoric
that speaks nothing of the rain
hauls shit, breaks his back so hard
the company applauds him
with more work hours
will come to his funeral.

My brother holds no dancing princess
in his hand
is a pallbearer of bee colonies
a scalded arm from my car radiator
grease monkey's handshake
goes around in his jeans, work boots
tries to jimmy god off a toothpick
can play a mean game of cards
fake a poker straight
shoot the moon
bid his last chips at Tripoly
for the chance of better hearts.

Every day something has hazarded
to cripple him.
Every day someone has secretly called
his name beyond aching.
Every year he has survived
his own diligence, drug addiction
like a boy on a string
baits death with his fish hook
till it comes.

# My brother is on the bandwagon

becomes brave after a beer
sings *Love me or Leave me*
as if some sassy girl is going to fuck with him
clean up his ways
offer bath salts in the middle of winter.

He has a terrible voice but who's saying.
Karaoke on a shoestring.
His saga of busted love held tight to his chest.
My mother's keepsake.

My brother is bandwagoning his love
for a call girl bride
some foreign beauty in love with simple things –
a walk in the woods, iced Pepsi
beach sand and jeep tracks.
She will not spit in his face
cause malignancy
not be a candidate for the debate team
nitpick the way he does dishes, fixes a sink

but like the shell of a walnut
will crack him open slow
lick the pooled oil
chamber by chamber
savor his good meat.

## In the speaker's cruise book

we are at a funeral
my brother's casket is closed
I try to be bright
talk up his past
his crazy antics on four wheelers
good heart that moped up disease
could fix a clock, car chassis
pad my brakes
make us laugh
till our pants wet,
recall his big hands that broke sweat
in hard jobs
begged overtime
never took vacation.

In the speaker's cruise book
I do not fall apart
show his celibate life in two videos
watch him soar on the motorcycle through wheat fields
jump ruts

his shoes fit —workman's boots
mud caked, tinged with the supplicate
of my mother's roses
are aerated with wings
no lasting dirt indebts them

the drug dealers never strangle
ditch him before the hospital
the woman with two kids who pretends to run a motel
keeps no plastic bags to bait his appetite

no one kicks in the front door at night
scares his housemate.
The rifle he borrowed for protection is not loaded.

In the speaker's cruise book
no threat stays firm
the durability of love keeps his heart green
pumps even blood into a poor man's sunset
he walks through summer fields
crawls into the arms of my mother
roots himself inside her paisley dress
wants for nothing but her scent
harbor of trees.

## My brother wears the only pair of jeans

he will ever know
the only tee shirt
his hands are crossed calm
as if all wrongdoing
urgency have slid away
and the day bends its knees
examines forsythia.

To cope with death
I scatter salt, scrub table
emery board my nails so short they bleed.

What age is the right age to die
what age signals a life too tired
to grow old here?
When we shuffle the cards at the family table
will my brother still look for the
queen of hearts, a sermon of aces?
What happens when the card dealer
the Russian roulette with a revolver fails?

My brother will never know a wedding processional
children's lunchboxes
yard where your dog poops
workbench in the garage for his tools
lawn mower, summer barbeques with hot dogs, kraut
a son's plea for ball practice
will never again listen to the hiss of a kitchen kettle
the way the chambers of the heart work in rhythm
push through the blood

the howl of a wolf
sound of hunger.

My brother wears the one pair of jeans
he will ever know.
They are lightly faded
sized for a tall, stocky man.
In the casket his feet are shoeless
as if an ocean waits
the sand won't scald.

His hands hold each other, filial twins
and finally, in his face
the slow song of an easy sky
drifts.

## My father will probably never know

the extent of hacked front doors and aerosol
that even the pins in my brother's leg cannot create
enough drag to swerve him.

We do not ever want to see tarnished what we love.
And what do the cops know about the way a dealer
can bury him for his piss off
land him in a tidied motel room with no shirt
his gold watch, expensive hoodie gone missing
glass of Pepsi beside the bed.

Better to put things in a plastic case, no autopsy
museum them to the dark.

For my brother every day had its dry ice to bear
shot gunned birds
as if willpower, coin operated machines
alone cannot save us.

Turn over a stone, and you are there
untangle the dark and we can hear you
call to us
exile our faithless …

And as for my brother's bright and shiny boy face –
dead or alive
it will always remind me of you

# We are damp

The rain keeps falling
indiscriminate
your desultory in my voice
the skunk cabbage willing themselves
into archaic thrones.
So much litter
and the sky refuses to come clean.

I want your cheap coffin to stand for something
its thin veneer, acetate folds
lost vernacular
the way your arms rest
one big hand folded over the other

as if you just changed spark plugs
scrubbed them
are resting on your providential
stalled over the lilies of the field
no more fretting
only a good night's sleep
a good night's sleep
before you haul yourself up and off to work.

You are in clean blue jeans, a simple tee
no holes, bare feet.
Your face looks peaceful
and I watch the way your hair slopes
its grey flecked fields
as if repose lays deep inside the sky's yearning
watch how these perky yellow and crimson roses
spill across the lid of your coffin
sing the other side of our loss.

I am making my final goodbye
will touch your lips, their bone chill
remember the way you slugged Pepsi
swore at injustice, fled from our mother's deathbed.

What can I say?
Do I plead *wait…come back..*
*do not do this to me*
although I know you are past listening
do I offer up a final kiss
reach beyond the sheltering makeup
uncreased brow
tell you the world will never be the same
never be the same

I do what any bereft sister might –
tuck in a sachet of lavender
love note to travel the centuries
one alabaster stone

let you take with you a cold hard
chunk of my heart

# Part Six

*St Lucia*

# The forensic light at the end of the world

of the world
could be my mother
her molten ash
silk kimono, oiled skin
that beckons the cottonwoods
to gleam even in winter.

The forensic light at the end
of the world
could be the foreground of
her Indian paintbrush
the fiery way her hand slaps black paint
banishes the ordinary
turns parlor walls *bohemian*
braids them in gold foil
late night on her step ladder
chain smoking British cigarettes.

The forensic light at the end
of the world
could be the flare and flame
of my brother's engines
ten years old, already a servant of wind
aerial handshakes
by sixteen wielding his own
black paint
turning his room into a bat cave
coiled snakes, green strobes
pot smoke.

The forensic light at the end
of the road

could be my father's fists turned into arrows
words that curl then flame
a house that burns so bright
it singes

makes us nimble
bright as a firecracker
as we fly through the sky
rescue lust from its blue pabulum

let nothing anchor
turn into a strangle.

The forensic light at the end
of the road
baths our mother, the lifeguard
in her cerulean sunset
Cape Cod sand
endless ocean

till we want to be thin, aerial, apostolic
scorch in her sun
watch her saunter in the slinky one piece
scissor the waves.

The forensic light at the end
of the road
can't be impaled on a toothpick
isn't a measure of sumo
the journeyman's suitcase
won't insure happiness for the new bride
save a drowning cat
absolve my father of his blue handcuffs.

The forensic light at the end
of the world
doesn't pretend to be my brother's best friend
hounds like store candy
the silver foil of my mother's  eye
watching him.

## My brother examines the preacher

his pronounced words and forbidden
his cleft lip
ordinary sing songs

examines the way death feels
not the abstract of it
culled by a sheepish mind
or abated with barbed wire fence line
but the *squeeze your ass*
*here I am* kind of affair
where the lips grow blue
and your heart empties
where there is no season of gulls
neat ecclesiastic.

My brother spot cleans the preacher
damp mops his brow
lets in strangers
the roughhewn and fractionalized

as if time is no sour puss
doesn't slaughter what it lends
travels us to some aptitude
where the weary grow into fish
every sunset is enough.

# My brother's courage

is more than a reliable handshake
reputation as the kickass worker
more than the back and forth he has traveled
to towns, cities across the continent
knowing no one, only his car, a twenty dollar bill
his wise crack jokes
tenacity in the face of our tattered American Dream.

My brother will never become a college professor
politician, radio announcer
never get past my father's razor sharp, my mother's death
will wear his past, his smarts discreetly
never marry his childhood sweetheart
rebuild another car
fix again my father's German cuckoo clock
feign a lousy hand
then slaughter us with his heart cards.

My brother will leave a hole in my life
the size of a house lot
as if something tender from the world has gone missing
and what we see, who we think we know
are only the tip of the iceberg -
he was more than his chorizo and frozen pizzas
pain over the hurting, down-on-their-luck
more than the boy inside the man
the embarrassed limp

was really a juggernaut
destined to defuse minefields
wrestle the dragon
debunk our ordinary
middle of the road box store
life in things.

## My brother is staying in St. Lucia

It is a late vacation.
He had to depart from here
with his life
for a vacation to be waiting.

I write him notes with the
slurred blue of my slush pen.
They have tulips pinned in the margin
a glimmer of spring
talk about Maggie the dog
my daughter's dance team
the way the light yields
to winter's clenched fist.

He says *the weather is good*
he walks a beach with sand
white as pearls
no longer limps
drinks watermelon juice from a coral cup
has slimmed down
is willing to wear a swimsuit
enter a restaurant
chat with the girls.

My brother has traveled to St. Lucia.
I send him a pint sized camera with lots of pixels
beg him to take pics - people, villages, sea life
make me a sketchbook
of what life after death
brings to him.

# Azalea

I want to let you know the azalea
I dug into the hard earth for you
a year ago February
is doing fine.

For a while last summer
I couldn't keep the roots moist
and the leaves dwarfed
brittle as fireweed
but something willed you back
blue sermoned you to stay.

I keep vigil
have watched you survive the pelting rain
of a Northwest winter
dry sticks that plague August

and now this April
in the unmown grass turned meadow
you have come back
sturdy as a perky bride
fan an arbor of bright new leaves
above the dark.

Chris, I hose you faithful

your green hands in the sun
a siren of glistening.

# Postscript

# Letter to My Brother

Dear Chris,

It's been a year since you died and I guess I'm supposed to believe things get easier. The hyacinth on the kitchen table slumps in its pot, scrawny green fingers, no petulance.

We had snow, mounds of it, so much ice the roads became almost peaceful. Maggie the dog was delirious, a trooper when we walked through the deserted neighborhood to the coffee place only to find it had just closed, then bribed Sonia to be teenage social, carried back two frozen pizzas from the empty shelves of the pharmacy.

I think of you a million times and not just your voice admonishing *get antifreeze*, think of your high stakes at the family card nights, carved whistles, the ballpark franks you loaded with spicy mustard, cheese whiz, your Buzz Lightyear, Felix the Cat impersonations

think of you in your cool shades on the phone saying *what? what?* as if I have to call for a reason or else it is boy troubles again, how you fielded the hard stuff I spilled at your door…listened, came to help me quick as a dime to watch the kids or see why my car key wouldn't turn

think of you building your yard ramps, riding through space on the dirt bikes, nine years old and already a servant of wind, precision aeronautics, how you could land on a patch the size of a stamp without skidding.

And did you like the raw terror as much as the applause, even after the months in hospital from the motorcycle accident,

even after you raised the stakes when mom died suddenly
went from pot smoker to something else….
did you like the raw terror
living on the edge …living on the edge…
holding tight to your ragged wing?

Toni Thomas lives in Portland, Oregon. Her poems have appeared in literary magazines in Austria, Spain, New Zealand, Canada, England, Scotland, and Australia. In the United States her work has been accepted for publication in over fifty literary magazines, including Prairie Schooner, North Dakota Quarterly, Hayden's Ferry Review, the Minnesota Review, Weber-The Contemporary West, Rhino, Notre Dame Review, and Poetry East.

She has published four other poetry collections – *Chosen, Fast as Lightning, Walking on Water* and *Blue Halo*. Her work has received numerous awards and twice been nominated for a Pushcart Prize.

When she is not writing poems, Toni enjoys sculpting clay. Her figurative pieces have been shown in gallery and museum exhibits in Portland and Chicago, displayed in literary magazines, and housed in private collections in the U.S. and England.

Since Toni remains buried in poems and manuscripts, she likes to imagine all of them out in the world thick as wild lupin swaying.

She can be contacted at www.tonithomaspoetry.com

www.ingramcontent.com/pod-product-compliance
Lightning Source LLC
Chambersburg PA
CBHW050542300426
44113CB00012B/2225